MW01643771

What The
History

THE TRAIL OF TEARS

Forced Relocation of Native Americans

Printed in the United States of America

First Edition: 2024

This copyright page includes the necessary copyright notice, permissions request information, acknowledgments for the cover design, interior design, and editing, as well as the details of the first edition.

www.littlebiggiant.com

INTRODUCTION

In the early 1830s, a tragic chapter unfolded in American history as thousands of Native Americans were forced from their ancestral lands in the southeastern United States. This harrowing journey, known as the Trail of Tears, saw the Cherokee, Creek, Seminole, Chickasaw, and Choctaw nations endure a grueling trek of over 1,000 miles, facing hunger, disease, and the bitter cold. As they marched westward to designated Indian Territory, many lost their lives along the way, their stories echoing through time. What drove this mass relocation, and how did it shape the future of a nation? The answers lie in the complex interplay of ambition, greed, and the relentless push for expansion that defined an era.

The Trail of Tears remains a haunting reminder of resilience and loss, inviting deeper exploration into the lives forever changed by this monumental event.

TABLE OF CONTENTS

CHAPTER 1

The Journey Begins: Understanding the Cherokee Nation and Their Land

Imagine a time long ago, before cars and smartphones, when the Cherokee people lived in harmony with the land, surrounded by the beauty of nature. The Cherokee Nation, one of the largest Native American tribes in the United States, called the rolling hills, sparkling rivers, and lush forests of the southeastern United States their home. They lived in what is now known as North Carolina, Georgia, Tennessee, and Alabama. Their villages were filled with laughter, stories, and a deep connection to the earth that nurtured them.

The Cherokee were skilled farmers, growing crops like corn, beans, and squash, which they called the "Three Sisters." These plants were like best friends, helping each other grow strong. The corn provided tall stalks for the beans to climb, while the squash spread out on the ground, protecting the soil and keeping it moist. The Cherokee understood that nature worked in harmony, and they respected the land that provided for them.

In addition to farming, the Cherokee were talented artisans. They crafted beautiful pottery, woven baskets, and intricate beadwork that told stories of their culture and traditions. Each piece was a reflection of their identity, much like how our favorite toys or clothes can show who we are. The Cherokee language, too, was a vital part of their culture. They created a syllabary, a system of writing, that allowed them to share their stories and history with future generations. This invention was like a key that unlocked the door to their past, preserving their heritage for years to come.

But as time went on, the Cherokee faced challenges. More and more settlers arrived, eager to claim the land for themselves. It was as if a storm was brewing, threatening the peaceful life the Cherokee had built. The settlers didn't understand the deep connection the Cherokee had with their land. To them, it was just a place to live and grow crops, but to the Cherokee, it was home—a sacred space where their ancestors had walked and their spirits still lingered.

In 1830, the United States government passed a law called the Indian Removal Act. This law forced many Native American tribes, including the Cherokee, to leave their homes and move westward to a new territory. It was a decision that shattered the lives of countless families. Imagine being told that you had to leave your beloved home, the place where you played as a child, learned from your elders, and celebrated your traditions. The Cherokee were heartbroken, but they knew they had to be brave.

As they prepared for their journey, the Cherokee gathered their belongings, their memories, and their hopes for the future. They traveled in groups, forming a long line of people, horses, and wagons. This journey would come to be known as the Trail of Tears, a name that evokes the sadness and pain of those who walked it. The path was not easy.

The weather was harsh, and food was scarce. Many Cherokee lost their lives along the way, their spirits joining the ancestors they had left behind.

But even in the face of adversity, the Cherokee held onto their culture and traditions. They sang songs, shared stories, and comforted one another, reminding themselves that they were not alone. Their strength and resilience were like a sturdy tree, bending but never breaking in the wind.

As we reflect on the Cherokee Nation and their land, we can't help but wonder about the importance of understanding and respecting different cultures. What can we learn from their connection to nature? How can we ensure that everyone's voice is heard, especially when it comes to protecting our planet and its people?

Key Takeaway: The Cherokee Nation teaches us the importance of respecting our land and each other. Their story reminds us that every culture has its own unique traditions and values, and it's our responsibility to listen, learn, and cherish these differences.

CHAPTER 2

The Indian Removal Act: What Prompted the Trail of Tears?

In the early 1800s, America was a land of dreams and possibilities, a place where people believed they could start anew. However, for many Native American tribes, this dream was becoming a nightmare. The government wanted more land for farming and settlement, and the beautiful lands of the Cherokee, Creek, Choctaw, Chickasaw, and Seminole tribes were seen as the perfect solution. This led to a heartbreaking decision that would change lives forever: the Indian Removal Act.

Imagine living in a cozy village surrounded by tall trees, sparkling rivers, and fields full of flowers. This was home for many Native Americans. They had lived on this land for generations, nurturing it and understanding its rhythms like a well-loved story. But as more settlers arrived, they brought with them a different way of life, one that often clashed with the traditions of the Native Americans. The settlers wanted to farm the land and grow crops like cotton, which was very valuable.

In 1830, President Andrew Jackson signed the Indian Removal Act, a law that would force thousands of Native Americans to leave their homes and travel to a new territory in what is now Oklahoma. This act was justified by the belief that it would allow for "progress" and the expansion of the United States. But at what cost? The Native Americans were not just numbers on a map; they were people with families, stories, and a deep connection to their land.

The decision to remove Native Americans from their homes was not made lightly. Many tribes tried to resist the removal, seeking help from the courts and the government. The Cherokee Nation even created a written language and a constitution, hoping to prove that they were a civilized society deserving of their land. Yet, despite their efforts, the government was determined to push them out.

As the leaves turned golden and the air grew crisp, the Native Americans faced a difficult choice: stay and fight for their land or leave everything behind for an uncertain future. Those who chose to leave began a journey that would become known as the Trail of Tears. Picture families walking for miles and miles, carrying their belongings, their hearts heavy with sadness. They faced harsh weather, illness, and hunger along the way.

The name "Trail of Tears" reflects the sorrow and suffering experienced by those who were forced to leave their homes. It was not just a physical journey; it was an emotional one, filled with loss and heartache. Children clung to their parents, and elders shared stories of their ancestors, reminding everyone of the beauty of their culture and the strength of their spirit.

Why did this happen? Was it fair to take away someone's home just because others wanted it? These questions linger like whispers in the wind. The Indian Removal Act was driven by a desire for land and resources, but it also revealed a darker side of humanity—a disregard for the lives and rights of others.

As we think about this chapter in history, it is essential to remember that every action has consequences. The Trail of Tears serves as a reminder of the importance of empathy and understanding. We must learn from the past to ensure that such injustices are never repeated.

Key Takeaway: The Indian Removal Act and the Trail of Tears teach us that our actions can deeply affect others. It's crucial to stand up for what is right and to treat everyone with kindness and respect, no matter their background or beliefs.

CHAPTER 3

Life Before the Trail: Cherokee Culture and Traditions

Once upon a time, in the lush green valleys and rolling hills of the southeastern

United States, there lived a remarkable people known as the Cherokee. Imagine a world where nature was not just a backdrop but a vital part of life, where every river, tree, and mountain held stories and wisdom. The Cherokee people lived in harmony with their surroundings, drawing strength and inspiration from the land they called home.

The Cherokee were skilled farmers, cultivating crops like corn, beans, and squash, which they called the "Three Sisters." Picture a vibrant garden filled with tall cornstalks swaying gently in the breeze, green bean vines climbing up the sturdy corn, and bright orange squash spreading across the ground. This special planting method not only provided food but also created a beautiful tapestry of life, showing how different plants could work together, just like a family.

But their connection to the land went beyond farming. The Cherokee believed in the power of storytelling, passing down their history and traditions through captivating tales. Elders would gather the young ones around a crackling fire, their faces illuminated by the warm glow. They would share stories of the Great Spirit, the creator of all things, and of the animals that roamed the earth, teaching valuable lessons about respect and balance. Can you imagine sitting there, wide-eyed, as the shadows danced around you, listening to tales of bravery and wisdom?

Art and craft were also essential to Cherokee life. They were talented artisans, creating intricate pottery, beautiful beadwork, and colorful woven baskets. Each piece told a story, reflecting their culture and the beauty of their surroundings. Imagine a basket woven from the finest reeds, each twist and turn forming a unique pattern, just like the stories of the people who made it. The Cherokee used these crafts not only for everyday life but also for ceremonies, celebrating the cycles of nature and the spirit of their ancestors.

Music and dance were the heartbeat of Cherokee culture. During special gatherings, families would come together to sing songs that echoed through the valleys, their voices blending like a sweet melody carried by the wind. Picture a joyful celebration, where everyone danced under the twinkling stars, their movements telling stories of their heritage. Each step was a reminder of who they were and where they came from, a beautiful expression of unity and love.

But life was not just about joy; the Cherokee faced challenges too. They had to navigate their relationship with other tribes and settlers who began to encroach on their lands. This struggle was like a storm brewing on the horizon, threatening to disrupt the harmony they had worked so hard to maintain. Yet, the Cherokee held on to their traditions and beliefs, finding strength in their unity and resilience.

As we explore the lives of the Cherokee before the Trail of Tears, we can see how their culture was a rich tapestry woven from the threads of nature, art, music, and community. Their way of life teaches us the importance of respecting the land and cherishing our connections with one another.

Key Takeaway: The Cherokee culture reminds us that our traditions and stories shape who we are. By honoring our roots and the world around us, we can create a brighter future together.

CHAPTER 4

The Long Walk: What Was the Route of the Trail of Tears?

Imagine a time long ago, when the trees whispered secrets to the wind, and the rivers sparkled like diamonds under the sun. This was the land of the Cherokee people, who lived in harmony with nature. They had homes, families, and a deep connection to the land that fed them. But one day, everything changed.

In the 1830s, the U.S. government made a decision that would change the lives of thousands forever. They wanted the land where the Cherokee lived, so they forced them to leave their homes and walk a long, painful journey to a new place called Indian Territory, which is now known as Oklahoma. This journey became known as the Trail of Tears.

Picture a long line of people, stretching as far as the eye can see. Men, women, and children walked together, carrying what little they could. The air was thick with sadness, and the sky seemed to cry along with them. The route they took was not a straight path; it twisted and turned like a winding river.

The journey began in the beautiful mountains of North Carolina, where the Cherokee had lived for generations. They traveled through the rolling hills of Georgia, where the sun set the trees ablaze with orange and gold. But this was not a joyful adventure; it was a forced march filled with hardships.

As they walked, the weather changed from warm sunshine to chilling rain. They crossed rivers that roared like angry lions, and trudged through muddy paths that sucked at their feet like quicksand. Some days, they were so hungry that their stomachs growled like wild animals, and they had to rely on the kindness of strangers or the small bits of food they could find along the way.

Along the route, many Cherokee fell ill or grew too weak to continue. It was a heart-wrenching sight to see families torn apart, as loved ones were left behind. The Trail of Tears was not just a physical journey; it was an emotional one, filled with loss and sorrow.

The path led them through the states of Tennessee, Alabama, and Mississippi, where they faced many dangers. They encountered wild animals, harsh weather, and sometimes even unfriendly people who did not understand their plight. Each step was a reminder of the homes they had lost, the lives they had left behind, and the uncertainty of what lay ahead.

Finally, after weeks of walking, they reached the Indian Territory. But even here, the struggle was not over. The land was different, and it took time for the Cherokee to rebuild their lives. They were resilient, like a flower pushing through the cracks of concrete, but the memories of the Trail of Tears would always stay with them.

This journey was a painful chapter in American history, one that reminds us of the importance of empathy and understanding. It teaches us that every person has a story, and every story deserves to be heard.

Key Takeaway: The Trail of Tears teaches us about the strength of the human spirit and the importance of respecting the homes and lives of others. It reminds us that we should always strive to understand and support one another, no matter where we come from.

CHAPTER 5

Facing Hardships: The Struggles of the Cherokee People

Once upon a time, in the lush green valleys and rolling hills of the southeastern United States, there lived a proud and resilient people known as the Cherokee. Their lives were woven together like the intricate patterns of a beautiful quilt, filled with stories, traditions, and a deep connection to the land. But the story of the Cherokee is not just one of beauty; it is also a tale of struggle, heartbreak, and the fight for survival.

Imagine waking up in a cozy home made of wood and clay, surrounded by your family. The sun rises, casting a golden light over the trees, and you can hear the birds singing their morning songs. This was the life of the Cherokee people before they faced unimaginable hardships. They lived in harmony with nature, growing crops like corn, beans, and squash. Their children played in the fields, and the elders shared wisdom around the fire. But as the years went by, things began to change.

In the early 1800s, the United States government, driven by the desire for more land, began to push the Cherokee and other Native American tribes off their ancestral homes. Imagine a powerful storm brewing on the horizon, dark clouds gathering, and the winds howling. This storm was not made of rain but of fear and uncertainty. The Cherokee were told they had to leave their beloved lands and move to a place far away, known as Indian Territory, which is now Oklahoma.

This forced journey was called the Trail of Tears, and it was anything but easy. Picture thousands of Cherokee people, young and old, setting out on a long, treacherous path. They traveled on foot, with only the belongings they could carry. The weather was harsh, with blazing sun during the day and freezing temperatures at night. Many were sick and weak, struggling to keep up with the group. Some had to leave behind their homes, their gardens, and the places where they had made memories.

As they marched on, they faced countless challenges. Rivers swelled with rain, making it difficult to cross. The ground was muddy and uneven, and many people fell ill. Imagine a mother holding her sick child, desperately trying to keep them warm while they camped under the stars. The nights were filled with the sounds of coughing and the cries of those who had lost loved ones along the way. It was a heartbreaking time, filled with loss and sorrow.

The Trail of Tears was not just a physical journey; it was an emotional one as well. Many Cherokee people felt a deep sense of sadness as they left behind the land that had nurtured them for generations. They had stories to tell, songs to sing, and a culture that was rich and vibrant. Yet, as they walked, they held onto hope. They remembered the words of their ancestors, who taught them to be strong and to persevere in the face of adversity.

When they finally arrived in Indian Territory, it was not the promised land they had hoped for. The land was unfamiliar, and they had to start anew. Imagine trying to build a life from scratch, planting seeds in soil that felt foreign, and learning to navigate a new environment. The Cherokee faced many hardships in this new land, but they did not give up. They came together as a community, helping one another and sharing their skills. They rebuilt their homes, their schools, and their lives, showing incredible strength and resilience.

Through their struggles, the Cherokee people taught us important lessons about courage, unity, and the power of hope. They faced tremendous hardships, yet they remained connected to their culture and traditions. Their spirit shone brightly, like a beacon of light guiding them through the darkest of times.

As we reflect on the struggles of the Cherokee, we can ask ourselves: How can we support those who are facing difficulties today? What can we learn from their story about standing together and helping one another? The story of the Cherokee reminds us that even in the face of great challenges, we can find strength in our communities and in our hearts.

Key Takeaway: The struggles of the Cherokee people teach us the importance of resilience and unity. Even in tough times, we can support one another and find hope together.

CHAPTER 6

The Role of the U.S. Government: Who Was Involved?

Imagine standing at the edge of a vast forest, filled with towering trees and the sweet sounds of birds singing. This forest is home to many creatures, but one day, people from a distant land decide they want to take that forest for themselves. This is similar to what happened to the Native American tribes in the early 1800s, when the U.S. government made decisions that changed their lives forever.

The U.S. government, which is like the big boss of the country, was responsible for many of the actions that led to the Trail of Tears. Key figures in this story include President Andrew Jackson, who was like a captain steering a ship through stormy waters. He believed that the land in the Southeast, where many Native American tribes lived, should be used for farming and settlement by American citizens. Jackson thought that moving Native Americans westward would be best for everyone, even though it meant uprooting entire communities from their homes.

Now, let's picture a young girl named Sarah, who lived in a Cherokee village. She played among the trees and listened to the stories of her elders. But one day, Sarah heard whispers of a plan that would force her family to leave their home. The government wanted to move her people to a place far away, where they would have to start over. Sarah felt a knot of fear in her stomach, knowing that the journey would be long and hard.

The Indian Removal Act of 1830 was the law that allowed this to happen. It was like a huge wave crashing onto the shore, sweeping away everything in its path. The law was passed with the support of many government officials who believed in the idea of "Manifest Destiny," which meant that Americans were destined to expand across the continent. They thought it was their right to take the land, but they didn't consider the feelings and lives of the Native Americans who had lived there for generations.

As Sarah and her family prepared for the journey, they were not alone. Many other tribes, including the Creek, Choctaw, and Seminole, were also affected. Each tribe had its own unique culture, traditions, and stories, but they all faced the same fate. The government, with its powerful army, began to force these tribes to leave their homes, often using violence and threats. It was as if a dark cloud had settled over their lives, blocking out the sun.

The journey to the new land, which was often in present-day Oklahoma, was grueling. Families had to walk hundreds of miles, sometimes in harsh weather conditions, with little food or shelter. Many people became sick, and sadly, many did not survive. Sarah's heart ached as she thought of the friends and family who had been left behind, and she wondered why the government had chosen to treat them this way.

In the end, the role of the U.S. government in the Trail of Tears serves as a reminder of the importance of understanding and respecting the rights of all people. It's crucial to remember that behind every decision made by leaders, there are real lives affected. Sarah's story is just one of many, and it teaches us that we must listen to each other and work together to create a world where everyone feels valued and safe.

Key Takeaway: The actions of the U.S. government during the Trail of Tears remind us that leaders must think about how their decisions affect the lives of others. It's important to treat everyone with kindness and respect, no matter where they come from.

CHAPTER 7

Stories of Survival: Remarkable Accounts from the Trail

The sun hung low in the sky, casting a golden hue over the vast expanse of land that stretched before the weary travelers. The Trail of Tears was not just a path; it was a journey filled with heartache, courage, and the unbreakable spirit of those who walked it. Imagine a long line of families, each one carrying the weight of their history on their backs, trudging through mud and rain, their hearts heavy with loss. This chapter tells the stories of those who faced unimaginable challenges yet found ways to survive against all odds.

One such story is that of a young girl named Sarah. She was only ten years old when her family was forced to leave their home in Georgia. With tears in her eyes, she looked back at the place where she had played, where the sunflowers bloomed in the summer, and where her laughter echoed through the trees. But there was no time for goodbyes. Soldiers were waiting, and the only choice was to march forward.

As Sarah walked along the dusty trail, she clutched her little brother's hand tightly. He was just a baby, and she promised to protect him no matter what. Days turned into weeks, and the journey grew harder. They faced cold nights that bit at their skin, and hunger gnawed at their stomachs like a wild animal. Sarah often shared her meager rations with her brother, whispering stories of their home to keep his spirits up. "One day," she would say, "we will find a place where we can laugh and play again."

Then there was the tale of a brave man named John, who was a skilled hunter. When his family was forced onto the trail, he vowed to find food for them. With nothing but a small knife and his wits, he ventured into the woods, searching for anything that could help. One night, under the blanket of stars, he spotted a deer grazing nearby. With a steady hand and a heart full of determination, he crept closer. The thrill of the hunt surged through him, but it was not just for sport; it was for survival.

After a tense moment, John made his move. The deer fell, and he felt a rush of triumph mixed with gratitude. He brought the meat back to his family, and they gathered around the fire, sharing the meal. For a moment, they forgot about the hardships of the trail and found comfort in each other's company. "We are still here," John reminded them, "and as long as we have each other, we will survive."

As the journey continued, there were many others who showed incredible strength. An elderly woman named Grandma Mary, with her silver hair and wise eyes, shared her stories of resilience with the younger ones. She would sit by the fire at night, telling tales of her ancestors who had faced struggles long before her. "Remember," she would say, "we are not just survivors; we are warriors of our people. Our stories will live on, no matter what happens."

But the trail was not just a test of physical endurance; it was a battle against despair. Many lost loved ones along the way, and the sorrow weighed heavily on the hearts of those who remained. Yet, even in their grief, they found ways to honor those who had passed. They would sing songs of remembrance, their voices rising like a prayer into the night sky.

These stories of survival remind us that even in the darkest times, hope can shine like a beacon. The journey of the Trail of Tears was filled with suffering, but it was also a testament to the strength of the human spirit. Each person who walked that trail carried a story—a story of love, loss, and an unyielding desire to keep going.

As we reflect on these remarkable accounts, we must ask ourselves: What does it mean to be resilient? How do we support each other in times of hardship? The answers lie in the stories of those who walked the Trail of Tears, reminding us that we are all connected by our shared experiences of struggle and survival.

Key Takeaway: Even in the toughest times, the strength of family, hope, and community can help us overcome challenges.

CHAPTER 8

The Impact on Families: How the Trail of Tears Changed Lives

Imagine a peaceful village nestled by a sparkling river, where families gather around warm fires, sharing stories and laughter. This was the home of many Native American tribes, like the Cherokee, who lived on the land for generations. They cultivated their fields, hunted in the forests, and created rich traditions that celebrated their connection to nature and each other. But in the 1830s, everything changed.

The Trail of Tears was not just a path through the wilderness; it was a journey filled with heartbreak and loss. The U.S. government decided to force the Cherokee and other tribes off their ancestral lands, claiming it was for their own good. However, this decision shattered the lives of countless families. Picture a mother holding her child tightly as they prepare to leave their home, knowing they may never return. The air is thick with sadness and uncertainty.

As families were forced to march hundreds of miles to a new, unfamiliar land, they faced harsh weather, hunger, and illness. Many people fell ill, and tragically, thousands did not survive the journey. Each loss was like a stone dropped into a still pond, sending ripples of grief through the community. Children lost parents, and parents lost children. Brothers and sisters were separated, and families were torn apart. The bonds that held them together were stretched thin, like a fragile thread about to snap.

The impact of the Trail of Tears didn't just stop with the journey; it changed the very fabric of their lives. Families who once thrived in their homeland now struggled to find their place in a new environment. Imagine arriving in a place where the trees look different, the soil feels strange, and the rivers don't sing the same songs. The Cherokee had to adapt to new ways of living, which was not easy. They faced challenges in farming, hunting, and even finding familiar foods. The memories of their homeland haunted them like shadows, reminding them of what they had lost.

One famous Cherokee leader, John Ross, fought tirelessly for his people. He wrote letters and spoke passionately, trying to protect their rights and land. But despite his efforts, the Trail of Tears became a reality. John Ross's heart ached for his people, and his determination to help them showed the strength of family ties and leadership in times of despair. He believed that even in the darkest moments, hope could light the way forward.

As the years passed, the effects of the Trail of Tears lingered like a distant echo. Families struggled to rebuild their lives, but the scars of their journey remained. They carried their stories in their hearts, passing them down through generations. These stories became a source of strength, teaching their children about resilience, courage, and the importance of remembering their roots.

The Trail of Tears was more than just a physical journey; it was a transformation that reshaped families and communities. It taught everyone involved about the power of love, loss, and the unbreakable bonds that tie us to one another. As we reflect on this painful chapter in history, we can ask ourselves: How do we honor the memories of those who came before us? What can we learn from their struggles and triumphs?

Key Takeaway: The Trail of Tears reminds us that families are like strong trees with deep roots. Even when faced with great challenges, love and connection can help us grow and find our way back to each other.

CHAPTER 9

Remembering the Past: The Legacy of the Trail of Tears Today

Imagine standing on a quiet riverbank, the water flowing gently beneath the warm sun. The trees around you sway softly in the breeze, their leaves whispering secrets of the past. This serene place holds stories that echo through time, stories of bravery, loss, and resilience. One of those stories is the Trail of Tears, a journey that changed the lives of many Native Americans forever.

In the 1830s, thousands of Native Americans were forced to leave their homes in the southeastern United States. This journey was not a simple walk in the park; it was filled with hardships and heartache. Families traveled for miles and miles, facing harsh weather, hunger, and illness. It was a time when hope felt as distant as the stars in the night sky.

Today, the Trail of Tears is not just a historical event; it is a powerful reminder of the struggles faced by Native American communities. When we remember this painful chapter in history, we honor the strength and courage of those who walked the trail. Each step they took was a testament to their spirit and determination to survive, even when the world seemed against them.

But what does the legacy of the Trail of Tears mean for us today? It teaches us important lessons about empathy and understanding. We live in a world where different cultures and backgrounds come together, and it's essential to recognize and respect each other's stories. Just like the river that flows, our lives are interconnected. When we learn about the past, we can better understand the present and shape a brighter future.

For example, many Native American tribes continue to share their stories and traditions, keeping their cultures alive. They hold gatherings, festivals, and ceremonies that celebrate their heritage. By participating in these events, we can learn from them and appreciate the richness of their cultures. Imagine joining a powwow, where the sound of drums fills the air, and colorful dancers swirl like leaves in the wind. It's a chance to connect with history and honor those who came before us.

As we reflect on the Trail of Tears, we must also think about our responsibilities. How can we ensure that such injustices never happen again? It starts with kindness and awareness. We can be advocates for those who may not have a voice and stand up against discrimination and unfair treatment. Each of us has the power to make a difference, no matter how small.

Moreover, remembering the Trail of Tears encourages us to appreciate the beauty of our diverse world. Just as a garden flourishes with different flowers, our society thrives when we embrace our differences. We can learn from one another, share our experiences, and grow together. This journey of understanding helps us build bridges of friendship and compassion.

In schools, children are taught about the Trail of Tears to ensure that the lessons of the past are not forgotten. Through stories, art, and discussions, students learn about the importance of empathy and the impact of their actions. They discover that history is not just about dates and events; it's about people and their experiences. By sharing these stories, we can inspire future generations to be more compassionate and aware of the world around them.

As we stand on that riverbank, listening to the whispers of the trees, we are reminded of the resilience of the human spirit. The Trail of Tears may have been a painful journey, but it also symbolizes hope and survival. It teaches us that even in the darkest times, we can find light and strength within ourselves.

Key Takeaway: Remembering the Trail of Tears helps us understand the importance of empathy, respect for different cultures, and the power of kindness. By learning from the past, we can create a better future for everyone.

CHAPTER 10

Lessons Learned: What Can We Take Away from This History?

As we sit beneath the vast, twinkling sky, let's take a moment to reflect on a difficult chapter in our history—the Trail of Tears. This event was not just a series of forced marches;

it was a painful journey that many Native American tribes, particularly the Cherokee, faced in the 1830s. Imagine being uprooted from your home, your garden, and your favorite tree, and then being made to walk for miles and miles to a place you didn't know. It's a story that teaches us about loss, resilience, and the importance of understanding one another.

The Trail of Tears began when the U.S. government decided that Native American tribes should leave their ancestral lands in the Southeast and move to a designated area in what is now Oklahoma. It was as if someone decided to change the address of a beloved family without asking them, ignoring their deep connection to the land. The Cherokee, who had lived in harmony with nature for generations, were forced to leave their homes, their schools, and their sacred places. Can you imagine the fear and sadness they felt?

As thousands of Cherokee and other tribes began their long journey, they faced terrible conditions. The weather was often harsh, with cold rain soaking their clothes and mud clinging to their shoes like a stubborn shadow. Many people fell ill, and some didn't survive the journey. Each step they took was a reminder of what they had lost. It was a time of great suffering, but also a time that showed the strength of the human spirit.

One of the most important lessons we can learn from the Trail of Tears is empathy. Empathy means putting ourselves in someone else's shoes and trying to understand their feelings. When we hear stories of hardship and struggle, like those of the Cherokee, we can learn to be kinder and more compassionate. We should ask ourselves: How would we feel if we were in their place? What would we want others to do for us?

Another lesson is the importance of standing up for what is right. The Trail of Tears was a result of decisions made by those in power without considering the impact on the lives of the Native American people. It reminds us that we must speak out against injustice, whether it's in our own communities or around the world. When we see something wrong, we can choose to be brave and take action.

Additionally, the Trail of Tears teaches us about the significance of preserving history. By remembering the past, we can honor those who suffered and ensure that such events do not happen again. History is like a giant puzzle, and each piece helps us understand who we are today. When we learn about the struggles of others, we gain wisdom that can guide our actions in the future.

As we reflect on this painful chapter, we must also celebrate the resilience of the Native American people. Despite the hardships they faced, many tribes continue to thrive today, sharing their rich cultures and traditions with the world. Their stories are not just about loss; they are also about survival, strength, and hope.

So, as we gaze at the stars and ponder our place in the universe, let us carry these lessons with us. Let's remember to be empathetic, to stand up for justice, and to learn from history. The world is a better place when we treat each other with kindness and respect.

Key Takeaway: The Trail of Tears teaches us the importance of empathy, standing up for what is right, and learning from history to create a better future for everyone.

DEAR READERS

Thank you for choosing "What the History"! We hope this book has ignited a spark of wonder and motivation within you.

If you found this book captivating and believe in the transformative power of its message, we kindly ask for your support. Please consider leaving a glowing review on the platform where you purchased the book. Your review will help spread this message of empowerment to even more young readers, inspiring them to dream big and reach for the stars.

The core essence of this book - to inspire and uplift young minds - is what truly matters. We acknowledge that perfection is elusive, and we appreciate your understanding and forgiveness for any minor imperfections.

Thank you for being a part of our mission to nurture the brilliance and potential within the next generation. Your feedback will go a long way in helping us continue to provide captivating and transformative stories for young readers.

Made in United States
Orlando, FL
20 February 2025

58734689R00056